A Message to the Man

A Message to the Man

Jarius Hayes

Printed in the United States of America
Keen Vision Publishing, LLC
www.publishwithKVP.com
ISBN: 978-1-948270-87-8

Dedicated to my beautiful wife, Candice and our children. Desiree', Kendall, and Caleb. Thank you for supporting me in everything I do.

Table of Contents

A Message to the Man

This book is a Manhood 101 manual. It will make you look introspectively into your soul about what type of man, Christian, father, and leader you are. It not only lays out what you should be progressing to as a man, Jarius Hayes lays out many poignant ways of how to go about doing it. This book should be a required read for men in all stages of life. There is something here for the teenager all the way to the grandfather. It is a great, practical, no nonsense book about the development of a man. Thank you for writing this.

Dr. Jimmy Shaw

Superintendent of Florence City Schools

A Message to the Man is the book the men of this generation are in dire need of. While reading this book, I was instantly reminded of things my father would tell me growing up. I am thankful for this book because it put me in remembrance of the lessons I may have overlooked because I was too young to understand. This book is a resource I feel should be gifted to every young man when he turns thirteen.

Artavious Birdsong

In his new release, *A Message to the Man*, Jarius Hayes wastes no time getting to the point of this book. It is clear he is a man on a mission to help other men be great. I was encouraged, inspired, and motivated to do better in every facet of my life. Thank You!

D'Andre Hines

This book is going to change the life of every man who reads it. I feel like this book should be a requirement for men's rite of passage into manhood. What I enjoyed most was the way the author communicated in a language I could understand. Many times, people go over your head when trying to teach you something. That wasn't the case in this book. I understood and am able to apply these lessons to my every day life. On behalf of every man across the world, thank you, Mr. Hayes!

Urell Richardson

I grew up with a strong relationship with my father. As I read this book, I chuckled because I remember my father teaching many of the lessons Jarius Hayes teaches in this book. I feel like this book is a great read for men who grew up without their fathers or strong male influence. A book could never fill the role a father plays in a child's life through a lifetime, but this book comes real close to it!

Jeremy R. Kelsey

Introduction

One day, I asked an elderly gentleman for advice about living a long life. He looked at me and said, "Whatever hardships you encounter in life, just keep going, and God's grace will carry you through." His statement made me realize that in life, we will experience trials, tragedy, and trauma, but no matter what we are faced with, we must persevere.

As men, there is one thing we all have in common. We have all had to persevere through troubling times. I remember watching my father persevere through sickness. I remember watching my pastor persevere through the ups and downs of ministry. As for me, I have had to persevere through many tests and trials throughout the course of my life.

Everything that I've gone through taught me what truly makes a man. It isn't his ability to dodge life's troubles. It isn't his ability to be perfect. What makes a man is his ability to persevere despite the unfavorable conditions he encounters in life. I want you to take a moment and think about all you have persevered.

You've had to persevere through trauma.

You've had to persevere through financial loss.

You've had to persevere through disloyalty.

You've had to persevere through the loss.

You've had to persevere through grief.

You've had to persevere through the disappointment.

You've had to persevere through failure.

You've had to persevere through illness.

You've had to persevere through heartbreak.

In spite of everything you have been through, you made it. *Some* of the things you made it through almost killed you, but *everything* you endured made you better. Whether you are rich or poor, black, white, or brown, there are things you have experienced in life that you would not wish on your worst enemy. For this reason, a number of men are in need of healing, restoration, direction, and encouragement. That is why I wrote this book.

As a man, you play a vital role in society. You are needed and necessary in your family, relationships, community, and career field. Sometimes, the weight of being a man can feel unbearable. People have expectations of us, but we don't always have the understanding we need to fulfill those expectations.

This book is designed to provide men wisdom and guidance in areas like, dealing with your emotions, marriage, discipline, and friendships, just to name a few. As you read this book, allow it to aid in your pursuit of the missing pieces in your life. My desire for you is that you will realize that everything you endured was God's way of preparing you to propel you into the greatest season of your life. No matter what you are going through, I hope that this book,

A Message to the Man, inspires you to wake up each day and keep showing up on the battlefield of life. Take these messages to heart and use them to build the life you desire.

MESSAGE ONE

Pursue Your Purpose

"Use me, God. Show me how to take who I am, who I want to be, and what I can do, and use it for a purpose greater than myself."

Dr. Martin Luther King Jr.

Dr. Martin Luther King Jr. was the epitome of a man who lived a life of purpose. He served and contributed to the lives of others more than his own. Every time Dr. King spoke, he shook the nation at its core. Some people loved him, and some people hated him. Neither love nor hate prevented him from fighting for the equality of the marginalized and ostracized. We all could glean from Dr. King's courage, vision, focus, and perseverance. His life's story is one from which we can take many lessons and apply them to our lives.

If you look around any room, whether it be a bedroom, classroom, or living room, you can define the purpose for everything in the room. In these rooms, there are beds, chairs, tables, desks, sofas, and lamps, respectively. We know the purpose of a bed, a chair, and lights. If you asked some men about their purpose in life, unfortunately, very few would be able to answer. Men must return to God's original intent for their lives to experience the peace, joy, and fulfillment God has planned for them.

But while he thought on these things, behold, the angel of the Lord appeared unto him in a dream saying, Joseph, thou son of David, fear not to take unto thee Mary thy wife: for that which is conceived in her is of the Holy Ghost.

"Then Joseph her husband, being just a man, and not wanting to make her a public example, was minded to put her away secretly. But while he thought about these things, behold, an angel of the Lord appeared to him in a dream, saying, "Joseph, son of David, do not be afraid to take to you Mary your wife, for that which is [b]conceived in her is of the Holy Spirit. And she will bring forth a Son, and you shall call His name

Jesus, for He will save His people from their sins."
Matthew 1:19-21 (NKJV)

In this passage, the angel of the Lord appears to Joseph, Jesus' earthly father, and reveals to him the purpose of his son. What would the world be like if every parent knew their child's purpose and, with God's instruction and wisdom, trained and prepared that child to live a life of purpose? Imagine the peace this world would experience if men knew their purpose at a young age and were placed in environments that cultivated that very purpose.

Purpose is defined as the reason a person, place, or thing exists. I genuinely believe many negative issues we deal with in life stem from a lack of understanding our purpose. When a man does not understand their purpose, they become a wanderer in life, going about aimlessly with no fixed course or goal. Take a moment to ask yourself this question: *Why has God placed me on this earth?* Purpose, in the life of a man, falls into one of four categories: undetected, neglected, rejected, accepted.

UNDETECTED

Several men have a unique purpose deep down on the inside of them that they have never discovered. Frustration sets in when you know there is more to your life than what you are experiencing. When your God-given purpose goes undetected, you will attempt to be fulfilled in life by substitutes instead of the real things.

REJECTED

Rejection is when you refuse to accept something or someone. It is also when something is dismissed as inadequate.

So many men dismiss their purpose because of a dollar figure, lack of notoriety, and comparison. When a person rejects the purpose for their life, they accept unhappiness, mediocrity, and underachievement.

NEGLECTED

Neglect is when you fail to care for something properly. Neglect is knowing and even being on the path to fulfill purpose, but you may be inconsistent, lazy, or unfocused. Adversity is one of the main reasons men neglect purpose. The trials and tests of life have a way of planting seeds of doubt in our minds. As men, we may often find ourselves wondering, "Maybe I'm not on the right path." Fulfilling purpose will never be an adversity-free path. However, you should not allow hardships to stop you from doing what God purposed you to do.

ACCEPTED

When we accept something, that means that we receive it willfully. When we fully accept God's purpose for our lives, we place ourselves on a path to potentially experience heaven on earth. Knowing that you are doing the very thing God put you on this earth to do gives you a sense of gratification that cannot be explained. When we accept purpose, we no longer search for counterfeits because we have found the real thing.

Men aren't designed to be idle or without a challenge. Men need something to work on. When a man feels he has no value, he becomes destructive to himself and those around him. Men commit ninety percent of crimes committed in the United States. Men who have no sense of purpose can sometimes be blind to the value of anything else.

HOW DO I DISCOVER PURPOSE?

1. *Pray.*
2. *Pinpoint what continuously stimulates your mind and emotions.*
3. *Believe that you are the answer to a problem.*
4. *Serve others.*
5. *Understand that purpose evolves.*

PRAY.

Jeremiah 33:3 says, "Call unto me, and I will answer thee, and show thee great and mighty things which thou know not." Through prayer, God will specifically reveal the purpose of your life. You must still go through a process to carry out your purpose, but God will show you the path to take in prayer.

"Before I formed you in the womb I knew you; Before you were born I sanctified you; I ordained you a prophet to the nations."

Jeremiah 1:5 (NKJV)

"See, I have this day set you over the nations and over the kingdoms, To root out and to pull down, To destroy and to throw down, To build and to plant."

Jeremiah 1:10 (NKJV)

Jeremiah was a young man when God told him who he was and what he was purposed to do. As men, we must discover God's purpose for our lives so that we won't spend years meandering through life, guessing and wishing but never truly becoming who God designed us to be. Prayer is about communicating with God. We don't just pray when something is wrong. Prayer is also a tool we use to get direction, insight, and wisdom from God about our lives.

WHAT CONTINUOUSLY AWAKENS YOUR MIND AND EMOTIONS?

Certain things really get your mind and emotions moving in a positive and productive way. Some ideas, goals, and visions cannot be shaken and consistently move upon your mind and heart. It is vital that you don't let those things die out. Pursue what interests you. It may just be the path that will lead you to a life of fulfillment and purpose.

BELIEVE THAT YOU ARE THE ANSWER TO A PROBLEM.

It is easy to see that this world is full of problems; however, there are answers to these problems. They are found in the hearts and minds of people. If we take a hard look at what is plaguing society today, we will find out that we have the solution to these issues. Becoming aware of this truth will help you become more aggressive about executing your ideas and sharing your insight.

SERVE OTHERS.

Serving others in any capacity can open your eyes to abilities you never knew you possessed. Serving others should not make you feel inferior or superior to anyone. Instead, it should give you a sense of satisfaction as you give yourself to others. It is through serving others that we can learn who we really are. Serving those who cannot repay us reveals what is in our hearts and our true motives.

UNDERSTAND THAT PURPOSE EVOLVES.

What you are doing today, you may not be doing tomorrow. Your purpose inevitably evolves as you mature. We must be able to recognize when the grace for a season has lifted, and it's time to shift. Grace can be compared to a Godly-empowerment or supernatural strength to do something. When we set our minds on carrying out God's purpose for us, He grants us the grace to do so in a manner that fits where we are in life. We must recognize when that grace is over, and it is time to move on. Here are three ways you can tell that your purpose has evolved, and it may be time to move forward.

1. You feel burnout, and rest does not solve it.
2. You no longer look forward to what you do.
3. You no longer have vision for where you are headed.

There was a time in my life when I worked a job I really didn't like. I would take off from this job every chance I got. I thought that if I took some time away, it would help how I viewed this job. I was grateful for the position, but it was not what I wanted to do for eight to ten hours daily. No matter how many days I took off, I still felt major burnout. It was time for me to make a change. When you realize that you are frustrated and dissatisfied with what you are doing, stop and seek God. He will lead you down the right path.

Life should be so fulfilling that you can't wait to participate or take part in what you do, especially when it relates to your career. As a man, understanding and living out your purpose gives you the satisfaction you can't find in anything else. Unfortunately, many men have settled for an occupation that has nothing to do with their God-given purpose. You can make good money but still not be in your God-given purpose. You can be popular but still not be in your God-given purpose. You can be involved in something for decades, but it could still not be your God-given purpose. Only your God-given purpose will have you looking forward to every day of your life with excitement and anticipation.

When we sense our purpose is shifting, the vision for where we are transitioning comes alive, while the vision for where we are begins to die. It is so important to have successors you can pass the baton to so they can take the vision forward when it is time for you to stop or move on to something else. Your purpose may not be forever, but for an appointed time. Be okay when you have gone as far as God is allowing you to go. Don't hold the next generation hostage because you refuse to recognize the shift.

As a man, not knowing your purpose is dangerous. When you don't know the purpose of a thing, misuse will surely take place. This will more than likely decrease the longevity of a thing. Think about it. If you don't properly understand the purpose of certain tools, you could use them incorrectly once and cause permanent damage. The same concept applies to your life. If you don't understand your life's purpose, you could misuse your time, energy, and resources. Additionally, you could find yourself in situations that shorten your lifespan or even cost you your freedom.

Men, I do not want us to miss out on having a successful, enjoyable, impactful, and legacy-filled life because we lack knowledge of our life's purpose. Pursue purpose relentlessly and live your best life.

NOTES

_____

_____

_____

_____

_____

_____

_____

_____

_____

_____

_____

_____

_____

_____

_____

_____

_____

_____

_____

_____

_____

_____

_____

_____

_____

_____

_____

MESSAGE TWO

Write the Vision

Vision animates, inspires, and transforms purposes into action.

Warren Bennis

Hindsight is good, insight is great, but foresight gives birth to the invisible. Vision can take you from what is not present to manifestation. Vision is being able to see beyond your present state and circumstances. Men can become trapped and feel like there is no way out of the mediocrity that they may be experiencing. When we get in this place, it's easy to become frustrated. Some even give up and accept this, as if this is all life can ever be for them.

Where there is no vision, the people perish: but he that keepeth the law, happy is he.

Proverbs 29:18 (KJV)

One of the meanings of perish is to stray—stray means to aimlessly move away from the right course or place. When a man has no vision for his life, it is a possibility that he will unknowingly stray away from the very thing he should be doing.

Show me a man with vision, and I will show you a man who is full of expectation and focus. Vision is like a light on a dark pathway, leading the way to destiny. Before a man can achieve anything, he must have a vision for it. If you ask any successful person about the key to their success, more than likely, they would say, " I saw myself becoming what I wanted to be before it actually happened." They saw themselves finishing school, starting the business, or having a wife and children before it came into existence.

HAVING VISION MAKES CERTAIN DECISIONS EASY.

When something or someone looks as if it can disrupt where you are headed, it should be easy for you to make the best decision for your life. Why should it be easy? You should not want any unnecessary baggage on your journey. The wrong people will add weight to your journey that will slow your progress. People you may have been close to in the past may not be good for your future. As men, we must be courageous enough to cut off people or things that complicate and frustrate the vision you have for your life. Cutting someone off does always mean the love is lost. Sometimes, it's about setting healthy boundaries so that they won't hinder you.

HAVING VISION HELPS YOU OVERCOME ADVERSITY.

Brothers and sisters, I do not consider myself yet to have taken hold of it. But one thing I do: Forgetting what is behind and straining toward what is ahead, I press on toward the goal to win the prize for which God has called me heavenward in Christ Jesus.

Philippians 3:13-14 (NIV)

Everybody has experienced something in life that was difficult to overcome, whether it was the loss of a loved one, health issues, relationship drama, or financial difficulties. Whatever you may have had to overcome, continue to press toward your goal and finish the race you started. When you focus on victory instead of adversity, victory is magnified, and adversity loses its power over your life.

HAVING A VISION GIVES YOU STRENGTH.

"So let's not get tired of doing what is good. At just the right time we will reap a harvest of blessing if we don't give up."

Galatians 6:9 (NLT)

Fatigue will set in and try to cause you to give up and abort your mission prematurely. When you abort your mission or, in this case, your vision, it can be challenging to resume when you realize your mistake. It is so important to stay on course even when everything within you wants to quit.

"For the vision is yet for an appointed time; But at the end it will speak, and it will not lie. Though it tarries, wait for it; Because it will surely come, It will not tarry."

Habakkuk 2:3 (NKJV)

Don't allow the delayed fulfillment of your vision to make you weary. We must trust the timing of God in any endeavor.

CHARACTERISTICS OF A MAN OF VISION

1. A man of vision is not passive.

2. A man of vision is not idle.

3. A man of vision is a thinker.

4. A man of vision is strategic.

5. A man of vision chooses relationships wisely.

A MAN OF VISION IS NOT PASSIVE.

A man of vision will do whatever it takes to pursue the vision God has shown him for his life. Passivity is not apart of his makeup. Failure can cause a man to become passive because of the emotions that often come with disappointment. Betrayal can cause a man to become passive because he trusted the person who turned their back on him. A passive man will cower wherever there is push back, closed doors of opportunity, setbacks, or disappointments. As a man, I encourage you never to let anything or anybody take away your tenacity, grit, hunger, or perseverance. Keep going until the task is finished. When we deny the temptation to be passive but embrace the need to dig in and stay strong, we position ourselves to become victors and not victims.

A MAN OF VISION IS NOT IDLE.

Idleness creates bad habits that rob us of time we could have used to pursue, create, and develop things for our future. Idleness is a set up to engage in unproductive activities that yield negative results. A man of vision does not avoid the work it takes to become successful. Idleness is just a nice word for describing laziness. A lazy man is a broke man, a physically and mentally unhealthy man, and an unproductive man who has nothing to offer anybody. A man should be an example others look to when it comes to keeping your hand to the plow and staying the course when things get tough.

A MAN OF VISION IS A THINKER.

In this chaotic and fast-paced world, we must settle down and take time to think. I am still amazed by the thoughts and ideas that come to my mind when I just get quiet and still. We should think before we speak, think before we plan, and think before we make a move. Thinking takes patience that men must learn to develop. As you look over your life, you can see that you could have avoided some of the mistakes you made if you thought before taking action. Do not allow anyone to put time deadlines on you that prevent you from thinking through a situation and getting a clearer picture. Most of our biggest financial mistakes are made because we buy things on an impulse instead of considering how a purchase might affect our financial future.

A MAN OF VISION IS STRATEGIC.

When you fail to plan, you are planning to fail. You have probably heard this statement numerous times in your life. It is good to have a vision, but you also need a strategy to accomplish your vision. A strategy is needed to navigate your way through this uncertain, unstable, and unpredictable world that we live in. A strategy will not guarantee a smooth ride in life, but it will help counter setbacks that you may experience along the way. When a man has a strategy or a well thought out plan for his life, he will not deviate from it when obstacles arise. Now I understand God's plan should be our main objective to discover in life; however, even with God's plan, we should have a God strategy to guide us along the way.

A MAN OF VISION CHOOSES RELATIONSHIPS WISELY.

A man can be so successful in many areas in his life but fail to choose his relationships wisely. Investing in the wrong relationship can cost him dearly. Who a man decides to enter into a relationship with (whether it be a friend, the person you chose to marry, or a business partner) determines his road to success. With the wrong relationships, his journey will be more difficult than it should be. With the right relationships, it will be easier for him to overcome the challenges he faces along the way to success. When we chose to be in relationships, we develop bonds with individuals that are sometimes not easy to break. Unfortunately, some relationships can be a hindrance instead of a help. I encourage every man to seek God in relationships. Don't be casually selective in whom you choose to connect with. The people you connect with should want to stand with you in the good times, as well as the storms of life. They should encourage you forward instead of holding you back.

A man of vision can see beyond today, tomorrow, next week, and even next year. A man of vision has the mentality that however long it takes to complete his mission, he is willing to persevere, even when it seems like nothing is happening. Vision will keep a man in expectation even when life contradicts where he sees himself in the future. Men, having a vision for our lives is the best way to safeguard some of the most valuable blessings God has given us: time, resources, and energy.

NOTES

_____

_____

_____

_____

_____

_____

_____

_____

_____

_____

_____

_____

_____

_____

_____

_____

_____

_____

_____

_____

_____

_____

_____

_____

MESSAGE THREE

Have Self-Control

A man without self-control is like a city broken into and left without walls.

Proverbs 25:28 (ESV)

One day, as I was running some errands, a guy got out of his car and came up to my car window, shouting and pointing his finger. He felt like I pulled in a parking spot he was headed to. I wanted to get out and handle this guy, but I sat there, didn't move, or say a word. He eventually got back in his car and left. Over and over in my mind, I played what would have happened had I confronted this guy. The situation would have probably gotten ugly and could have been damaging to my life and his. That one moment of losing control of my emotions could have had lifelong consequences. Self-control is needed in our relationships, the workplace, and our day to day interaction with others. We must be able to see possible outcomes before an outburst.

Self-control is the ability to control one's desires and emotions. A man must be able to control his desires and emotions long enough to make quality decisions. When you allow your feelings and wants to rule your life, they can ruin your life. We must exercise self-control in every area, no matter the situations in which we find ourselves. One moment of not exhibiting self-control could destroy your whole life.

Self-control is not just about refraining from doing bad things but also overindulging in life's pleasures. Overindulgence of pleasures can cause you to lose focus on what is truly important. You can control what you think, what you say, and how you act. Lacking self-control will always position you to follow instead of becoming a leader. Out of control emotions and desires leads to an out of control life, which leads to consequences you have no control over.

In the Bible, King David was a man after God's heart, and he did great things. However, King David was also a man who could not control his desires. As men, we cannot allow our lack of self-control to diminish our greatness.

"Late one afternoon, after his midday rest, David got out of bed and was walking on the roof of the palace. As he looked out over the city, he noticed a woman of unusual beauty taking a bath. He sent someone to find out who she was, and he was told, "She is Bathsheba, the daughter of Eliam and the wife of Uriah the Hittite." Then David sent messengers to get her; and when she came to the palace, he slept with her. She had just completed the purification rites after having her menstrual period. Then she returned home. Later, when Bathsheba discovered that she was pregnant, she sent David a message, saying, "I'm pregnant.""

2 Samuel 11:2-5 (NLT)

Whatever you feed will continue to hunger for more of what you feed it. Whatever you starve will eventually die out. King David was feeding his desire for Bathsheba as he gazed upon her washing herself. The more he looked upon her, the more he desired her. Self-control is the ability to deny what looks and feels good to you if it is not good for you. When King David finds out Bathsheba is pregnant, his mind shifts into cover-up mode. Men, we cannot allow a bad decision to lead to a cover-up because it only digs a deeper hole in an already bad situation.

"So the next morning David wrote a letter to Joab and gave it to Uriah to deliver. The letter instructed Joab, "Station Uriah on the front lines where the battle is fiercest. Then pull back so that he will be killed."

So Joab assigned Uriah to a spot close to the city wall where he knew the enemy's strongest men were fighting. And when the enemy soldiers came out of the city to fight, Uriah the Hittite was killed along with several other Israelite soldiers."

2 Samuel 11:14-17 (NLT)

David's lack of self-control caused him to kill a man who had done nothing wrong. David allowed his desires to rule at this moment, and he ruined a life.

Lack of self-control didn't just impact David, but the generations that followed him. The Lord used Nathan, the prophet, to speak to David about his behavior's generational impact.

"Why, then, have you despised the word of the Lord and done this horrible deed? For you have murdered Uriah the Hittite with the sword of the Ammonites and stolen his wife. From this time on, your family will live by the sword because you have despised me by taking Uriah's wife to be your own."

2 Samuel 12:9-10 (NLT)

The drama continued in the family of David because of the seed sown to fulfill his ungodly desires. His son, Amnon, committed rape and incest and was murdered by David's son, Absalom. Later, Absalom led a revolt in an attempt to be king. (2 Samuel 16-17) Absalom was eventually murdered.

Solomon, who was also David's son, became a wise king. Unfortunately, just like his father, Solomon lacked self-control, which led to the kingdom being torn from him. The absence of self-control not only affects us but our family and the generations to come.

I've never understood why young ladies are frowned upon for being promiscuous, while young men are celebrated for this type of behavior. Young ladies have ceremonies to celebrate their commitment to saving themselves for marriage, but I hardly ever see ceremonies celebrating young men for doing the same. It seems that we teach our young ladies the value of walking in purity but forget to include young men in the conversation. We use the excuse, "Boys will be boys," to permit young men to live out of control. Young men can't get pregnant, but they can suffer emotional and psychological damage and contract STDs. When young men get older, they will choose wives based on sexual experience and not true love if they weren't taught self-control. In some cases, they may choose someone who is not compatible spiritually or with the purpose and vision for their lives.

MONEY

Listen, I am far from a financial expert, but I know how dangerous it is to lack self-control when it comes to your money. Whether you have a little or a lot, you must practice self-control. A man who lacks self-control in his finances remain broke and in debt. When you have money but lack self-control, you will always find yourself in lack. Lacking necessities, behind on bills, unhappy, and even spending money on drugs and alcohol to cover up unresolved issues. Regardless of how much money you have or don't have, money can be a self-destructive weapon that can lead you down a path of defeat without self-control. We cannot allow the love of money or the wrong relationship with money to cause our lives to be thrust into chaos and drama. I truly believe that money management classes should start as soon as young men are able to count and last throughout high school. As men, we should be masters of money rather than slaves to it.

ANGER

Even though we don't always like to acknowledge them, men also experience emotion. Perhaps the most common emotion among men is anger. As with all feelings, we must know how to control our anger. Unfortunately, many men struggle to manage their anger well. There will be moments when we experience anger. However, we must not allow anger to determine how we make decisions and treat others. Uncontrolled anger could put you on a very destructive path to irreversible damage.

In Numbers 20:4-5, the children of Israel were angry at Moses because they felt he led them to the wilderness to die. They had been traveling, and there was no water. Moses, in turn, became angry with the children of Israel and their never-ending complaints.

"You and Aaron must take the staff and assemble the entire community. As the people watch, speak to the rock over there, and it will pour out its water. You will provide enough water from the rock to satisfy the whole community and their livestock."

Numbers 20:8 (NLT)

Moses was given clear instructions to speak to the rock before the people, and the water would come forth. However, Moses' anger with the children of Israel blinded him of God's instructions.

"Then he and Aaron summoned the people to come and gather at the rock. "Listen, you rebels!" he shouted. "Must we bring you water from this rock?" Then Moses raised his hand and struck the rock twice with the staff, and water gushed out. So the entire community and their livestock drank their fill. But the Lord said to Moses and Aaron, "Because you did not trust me enough to demonstrate my holiness to the people of Israel, you will not lead them into the land I am giving them!""

Numbers 20:10-12 (NLT)

God instructed Moses to speak to the rock, but he smote the rock and disobeyed God out of anger. Moses' disobedience due to anger disqualified Moses from leading the children of Israel to the promised land.

"But go up to Pisgah Peak, and look over the land in every direction. Take a good look, but you may not cross the Jordan River. Instead, commission Joshua and encourage and strengthen him, for he will lead the people across the Jordan. He will give them all the land you now see before you as their possession.""

Deuteronomy 3:27-28 (NLT)

Moses was only able to see what he should have been able to experience. As men, we cannot allow anger to put us in a position where we cannot experience what God has provided.

As you can see, a lack of self-control in any area of your life can be detrimental to your future. As a man, make it your business to learn self-control. Be honest with yourself. Pray and ask God to reveal the areas where you lack self-control. Search for mentors and accountability partners who can provide you with wise counsel. Trust the voices God places in your life to help you when you lose your way. As you learn to practice more self-control, your life will become more fruitful, productive, and pleasing in the eyes of God.

MESSAGE FOUR

Choose the Right Environment

You are a product of your environment. So choose the environment that will best develop you toward your objective. Analyze your life in terms of its environment. Are the things around you helping you toward success - or are they holding you back?

W. Clement Stone

As a young man growing up, whenever I left the house, my dad always demanded to know where I was going. Of course, as a teenager, I didn't always like to have to answer him. Now that I am a man, I fully understand why it was important for my father to know where I was headed. He wanted to know the environment that I would be surrounding myself with.

Unfortunately, some men grew up in homes where no one cared. They were able to go wherever, whenever, and with whomever. As a result, many landed themselves in circumstances that were difficult to get out of. The environment that you consistently place yourself in can make you or break you. An environment can make you into something great or break you into fragments, causing you to be broken throughout your life. Our environments shape what we think and believe about ourselves and others. This is why it is vital to be exposed to healthy environments.

When I was in high school, my football coach took us to an NFL (National Football League) game. It had always been a dream of mine to one day play in the NFL. We went to Atlanta to see the Dallas Cowboys play the Atlanta Falcons. As I was watching the game, I imagined myself being on the field playing in the game. The excitement in the stadium was like nothing I had ever experienced. Do you want to know what happened while I was sitting there? Being exposed to that environment connected with a desire in my heart, causing me to not only dream, but also work towards achieving my dream. Five years later, I returned to that stadium, but this time, I was on the field playing against the Atlanta Falcons as an Arizona Cardinal.

EXPOSURE

The right exposure can change your life, while the wrong exposure can destroy it. Exposure can lead to observation, infatuation, and participation. Observation is when you look intently at what is going on around you. Through observation, you can determine quickly if the environment is conducive to your purpose, personality, or what you believe. At times, as men, we find ourselves in environments and become comfortable in places we should flee. Observing an environment will either feed your desires or quickly reveal that this is an environment you must disconnect from. Unfortunately, we often stay in certain environments because of our personal relationships with people in that environment instead of looking at the bigger picture. As men, we must be diligent about pinpointing what is beneficial and what is not right away; time is of the essence and cannot be wasted.

Infatuation is when you fall in love with something or someone right away. Becoming infatuated with an environment could be a good thing or a bad thing, depending upon whether the environment is positive or negative. It is very possible to become infatuated with a negative environment, especially when there are no standards set in your life. Becoming infatuated with a positive environment, on the other hand, is a great thing and could cause positive change in your life.

Men must watch what they participate in. Participation in any environment reveals that you believe that it is worth your time and energy. Participation is the breeding ground for consistency. The more we participate in something, the more we will continue to do it.

SHIFTING THE MOMENTUM

The right environment can shift the stagnant momentum you may be experiencing in your life. You may feel like things are at a standstill in your life. However, when you get exposed to a certain environment, things will start moving. The right environment can cause you to believe again where you once doubted. The right environment can cause you to put action behind your words and dreams. The right environment can revive a vision that you almost allowed to die. The right environment can cause you to start being more optimistic than pessimistic.

In a game of sports, a team could be losing horribly until something happens and shifts the game's momentum. A momentum shift can make a losing team unstoppable. I challenge you to find the right environment that will shift your losing mentality into a winning mentality. When you are exposed to an environment that causes a positive shift in your life, you become a conduit to create environments where others can come and experience a renewed hope in their life. Before you move into the next chapter, ask yourself these questions:

What tone do I set for the environment in my home?
Do I make my work environment better or worse?
How do I respond when I sense tension in certain environments?
Is God pleased with the environments I consistently place myself in?
Do my environments encourage me to produce or be lazy?

Spend some time assessing your current environment. Review the impact your environment has made on your life. Even if you grew up in an environment that wasn't positive or cannot get out of the environment you find yourself in, after reading this book, you will be equipped to make the changes you need to make mentally. Our environments can gradually build us up or quickly tear us down. What your eyes see, what your ears hear, and what your mind thinks determines where our lives go. Make sure that your environment aligns with what you say you desire out of life.

NOTES

MESSAGE FIVE

Be Restored

The Lord is my shepherd. I have all that I need. He lets me rest in green meadows; he leads me beside peaceful streams. He renews my strength. He guides me along right paths, bringing honor to his name.

Psalm 23:1-3 (NLT)

Two men pulled up to an abandoned house with an old rusty 1965 Chevy Impala parked in front of it. One of the men wanted to tear down the house and take the car to the local junkyard. The other man looked at the house and car and said he believed he could restore the car and house to their original state. One man saw junk while another man saw potential restoration.

One of the key factors to experiencing personal restoration is seeing yourself through the eyes of God. Through our own eyes, the mistakes and bad decisions we have made make it hard to see that we are worthy of restoration. Some men feel they deserve the unfortunate events that have happened to them as pay back for what they have done. If you are one of those men, I pray that you realize that the grace of God can restore your life to what God originally intended.

"Then the angel of the Lord came and sat beneath the great tree at Ophrah, which belonged to Joash of the clan of Abiezer. Gideon son of Joash was threshing wheat at the bottom of a winepress to hide the grain from the Midianites. The angel of the Lord appeared to him and said, "Mighty hero, the Lord is with you!" "Sir," Gideon replied, "if the Lord is with us, why has all this happened to us? And where are all the miracles our ancestors told us about? Didn't they say, 'The Lord brought us up out of Egypt'? But now the Lord has abandoned us and handed us over to the Midianites." Then the Lord turned to him and said, "Go with the strength you have, and rescue Israel from the Midianites. I am sending you!""

Judges 6:11-14 (NLT)

When the angel of the Lord appeared unto Gideon, he was threshing wheat so that they could hide it from the Midianites. In battles and wars, a common strategy is to destroy the opponent's crops and land. This weakens the city, and if you can weaken the city, you increase your chances of winning the battle. Gideon was afraid of the Midianites, but the angel of the Lord called him a mighty man of valor. Valor means strength and courage. God spoke to Gideon through how he saw Gideon, not by how Gideon saw himself. God told Gideon that he would save Israel from the hand of the Midianites. It was a process, but Gideon eventually saw himself through God's eyes and did exactly what God said he would do.

You may look at yourself as a failure, but God is calling you a success. You may look at yourself as a follower, but God is calling you a leader. You may have a hard time keeping a job, but God sees you as a businessman. Asking God how he sees you will put you on a path of complete restoration.

"The Lord says, "I will give you back what you lost to the swarming locusts, the hopping locusts, the stripping locusts, and the cutting locusts. It was I who sent this great destroying army against you."
Joel 2:25 (NLT)

For years, many of you reading this book haven't experienced peace and enjoyment in several areas of your life. You don't know what it feels like to be financially free, physically and mentally healthy, and drama-free in your relationships. However, I genuinely believe that it is time for men worldwide to make a comeback. The time has come for you to be restored as if the setbacks never happened.

You may be thinking...

I wish I finished high school.

I wish I finished college.

I wish I had not gotten into the car with those guys at 13.

I wish I didn't get kicked off the team my sophomore year in high school.

I should have accepted that scholarship.

I shouldn't have allowed my friends to talk me into getting high.

Where would my life be if I had stuck with my ex-girlfriend, who was beautiful and smart?

How would things be if I had gone to the doctor sooner?

Why didn't I talk to somebody before I made a decision?

What if my mom and dad didn't divorce?

Would my life be different if my mom had not given me away?

Where would I be if I had started exercising last year?

I should have listened to my ex-wife when I was married to her.

I should have listened to my pastor's sermons instead of going to sleep.

How much further would I be in my career if I didn't try to fight my supervisor at work?

What if I would have stayed home instead of going to that girl's house when her parents were away?

Very often, when we think about making a change in our lives, we are filled with regret for everything we did wrong. If we aren't careful, that regret can cause us to remain stagnant and never experience restoration. Be encouraged, my brother. God can restore and redeem you if you yield to Him.

"Three days later, when David and his men arrived home at their town of Ziklag, they found that the Amalekites had made a raid into

the Negev and Ziklag; they had crushed Ziklag and burned it to the ground. They had carried off the women and children and everyone else but without killing anyone. When David and his men saw the ruins and realized what had happened to their families, they wept until they could weep no more."

1 Samuel 30:1-4 (NLT)

David and his men were devastated. Ziklag was burned, and their wives, sons, and daughters were taken. Can you imagine what was going on in David and his men's minds and emotions? They had no idea what happened.

"David was now in great danger because all his men were very bitter about losing their sons and daughters, and they began to talk of stoning him. But David found strength in the Lord his God."

1 Samuel 30:6 (NLT)

As a man and leader, David knew that he had to overcome the feeling of devastation for restoration to take place. Instead of accepting defeat and throwing in the towel, David began to encourage himself in the Lord. As men, when life gets complicated, we must encourage ourselves in the Lord so that the people who depend on our leadership have an example to look to in tough times. We cannot allow our past trials and tests to cause us to draw back. Instead, we must allow God to strengthen us to overcome.

"Then David asked the Lord, "Should I chase after this band of raiders? Will I catch them?" And the Lord told him, "Yes, go after them. You will surely recover everything that was taken from you!"

1 Samuel 30:8 (NLT)

My prayer is that all men will experience a full recovery in every area of their lives. God wants to fix the broken pieces of your life. Broken men produce broken families that yield broken individuals who live broken lives. Though many would never reveal it, a lot of men feel like they are damaged goods. They feel like they have made such a mess of their lives that things are beyond repair. So many men have been living in condemnation for years. In many cases, men deal with things in silence and never open up about what may be troubling them. Men, we must be courageous enough to confront these issues in order to experience breakthrough and restoration. Restoration leads to:

- A fresh outlook on life
- 180-degree turnaround
- Getting the positive attention of others
- Recognizing the power of God

NOTES

MESSAGE SIX

Resist Jealousy

Noble hearts are neither jealous nor afraid because jealousy spells doubt and fear spells pettiness.

Honoré de Balzac

Men tend to compare themselves to other men. They compare their finances, careers, houses, cars, and even families. When men compare themselves to other men, that is an indicator that they are discontent in their current circumstances. For some men, regardless of what they have and have accomplished, they still feel like they haven't done enough.

I understand not being complacent and always striving to be better. However, a man should feel good about himself without having to feel like he has to outdo someone else. Comparison is an open door for jealousy to come in and wreak havoc. Jealousy has broken up friendships, caused conflict among siblings, and destroyed marriages. As men, we cannot allow jealousy to become a part of our lives. It can take our focus away from what matters. Jealousy takes up space in your mind and drains your emotions.

Men should be able to celebrate other men and learn from them. Could it be that God places other successful men around us so that we can envision ourselves being successful? Recognizing the success of another man does not take away from our manhood.

"David asked the soldiers standing nearby, "What will a man get for killing this Philistine and ending his defiance of Israel? Who is this pagan Philistine anyway, that he is allowed to defy the armies of the living God?" And these men gave David the same reply. They said, "Yes, that is the reward for killing him." But when David's oldest brother, Eliab, heard David talking to the men, he was angry. "What are you doing around here anyway?" he demanded. "What about those few sheep you're supposed to be taking care of? I know about your

pride and deceit. You just want to see the battle!"

1 Samuel 17:26-28 (NLT)

Goliath demanded the armies of Israel to choose a man to fight him. David inquires about what would be done to the man who kills Goliath the Philistine. Eliab gets angry at David for speaking to the men about this. Why was Eliab angry at David? I genuinely believe Eliab's anger was due to jealousy. You see, in an earlier passage of scripture, 1 Samuel 16, God sends his prophet, Samuel, to anoint one of the sons of Jesse. Eliab, being the oldest, probably thought he would be anointed as the new king. However, Samuel anointed David. I believe this triggered Eliab to become jealous of his younger brother. When another man gets a promotion that we thought belonged to us, it can be a crushing blow. How we respond to disappointments like these reveal our true character.

From 1992-1995, I played football for the University of North Alabama. During those years, we won three national championships in a row, from 1993-1995. In three years, we only lost one game. Needless to say, we were pretty good. I remember walking around campus one day in between classes, and a guy I knew came up to me and said, " Hayes, you are walking around here like you somebody special."

I laughed and played it off, but the look in his eyes told me he was not joking around. I walked away, but his statement made me think. I had known that guy for a very long time, and I couldn't understand why he made that statement. We had never had any run-ins or confrontations. In my mind, he didn't have a reason to be jealous of me, but he apparently was. He was jealous of the attention I received from being on a great football team, but he had no idea the commitment and sacrifice it took me to make it to that point of my life. If he really knew my story, he would have been celebrating me instead of being jealous. Romans 12:15 tells us, "Rejoice with those who rejoice, and weep with those who weep." Rejoicing when others experience success casts out the spirit of jealousy that often tries to rear its ugly head in our hearts. Let's discuss three reasons why some men battle with jealousy.

UNDERACHIEVEMENT

Another word for someone who is jealous is the word *hater*. I'm sure you've heard that term before. A hater is typically someone who cannot celebrate the success of others. The thing that most haters have in common is the fact that they have underachieved in many areas of life. Underachievement is when a person does not reach their full potential based on the ability God has blessed them with. Deep down inside, they know they could have accomplished more, and it eats away at their confidence daily. Underachievement can cause you to become bitter, regretful, and jealous of others.

Distractions could cause underachievement. Distractions come in many forms and can prevent you from being your best self. Anything or anybody that takes your attention away from something is a distraction. Distractions deceive you into thinking that what you are distracted by is more important than what you should be focused on. That deception turns into disinterest. When we become disinterested, we are no longer excited about completing what we originally started. When we become disinterested in our goals and dreams, we never reach our full potential; therefore, we become underachievers.

FEELING LIKE ONE WAS MORE QUALIFIED THAN THE INDIVIDUAL GIVEN THE OPPORTUNITY.

We've all been here at least once in our lives. We see someone half as good as us flourishing, and we think to ourselves, "I was just as qualified or better than they were. That should be me." Sometimes, life will throw situations at us that don't make sense. In these moments, we cannot allow jealousy to linger in our hearts. We may feel more deserving of the award, promotion, or recognition, but we should still celebrate whomever it was given to. Understand that you will never win if you quit or keep your eyes on another person's lane. Always be okay when others are elevated, and trust that God will increase you at the right time.

BEING SURPASSED BY THOSE YOU STARTED WITH.

Feeling left behind by those we were once on the same level with is one of the biggest reasons we struggle with jealousy. When those around you achieve success quicker than you, it can shake you up a little bit. It will make you wonder, "Well, dang. What am I doing wrong?" As men, we should always want to be around people who are ascending so that we won't get comfortable settling for less than God's best. Learn from men who continue to soar to new heights so that you can too. Besides, if you are the smartest, most successful, and most productive person in your crew, you need to find a new crew.

If we aren't careful, jealousy can become our downfall. When feelings of jealousy try to overcome you, take a step back and allow yourself to put things in perspective. Instead of speaking badly about another individual, ask yourself, "Why does their success bother me so much?" Be honest and real with yourself. Is it because you know you could be doing more? If that is the case, get more productive. If the individual is close to you, glean from their wisdom instead of coveting their success. Don't allow jealousy to make you miss the lessons that could take you to the next level.

NOTES

MESSAGE SEVEN

You were not Meant to be Average

Very truly I tell you, whoever believes in me will do the works I have been doing, and they will do even greater things than these, because I am going to the Father.

John 14:12 (NIV)

Being average to some people can be a relief. Why? When you have been struggling, down and out, experiencing trial after trial, and you reach a certain level in life, it's normal to crave the familiarity of your previous level. However, we must understand that our previous level was meant to be a pit stop, not the final destination. The storms of life and the adversity we experience can take so much out of us that we think being average is greatness.

Yes, we should be grateful for what we have and where we are in life. However, don't be deceived into thinking that you have reached the pinnacle of your life. There is more for you ahead.

You were not meant to live an average life. A lot of the depression, frustration, and anger men deal with is the result of knowing there is more to life than what they have achieved. Average is just enough or just getting by. Greatness should be what every man wants to obtain in every area of his life. A man should not want to be a great father and an average husband. A man should not want to be in a great situation financially but be poor in health. A man should not allow average to be part of his thinking or his vocabulary.

WHAT IS THE PROBLEM WITH BEING AVERAGE?

BEING AVERAGE IS CONTAGIOUS.

The term contagious is normally used in reference to a disease/sickness that has the ability to spread from one person to another. Being average is just as life threatening as a deadly virus. Being average can spread from you to others who are highly influenced by you. Being average can spread to your family, your coworkers, and if you are a business owner, to your employees. Your mediocre attitude and how you approach things can quickly spread, and you will find yourself surrounded by average instead of greatness.

The spirit of average can take root in your life and require years to uproot out of your life and others. Being average sets a standard in your life that will affect everything around you.

BEING AVERAGE ROBS YOU OF OPEN DOORS OF OPPORTUNITY.

When people look for a certain skill, service, or employee, they, at times, might settle for average but people want greatness. When you have not been developed to a level of greatness, a possible open door can be closed shut. Average men place blame on others when doors of opportunities are shut instead of taking a look in the mirror and making the changes that need to be made.

BEING OKAY WITH BEING AVERAGE STOPS YOUR DEVELOPMENT.

When you feel like you have arrived and reached a certain level of success, you will not have a sense of urgency to continue to develop as a man. Development should be a mindset a man should have as long as he has breath in his body. Develop in the areas of your life where there are weaknesses, and you will experience a fresh new outlook in life that you have never experienced.

I talk about sports a lot because it was such a big part of my life. As a young boy starting out in organized sports, I always wondered why the coaches were so hard on players, even at a young age. As I got older, I understood why. If you don't demand greatness, you will never get it. Greatness is not being the next Michael Jordan or Lebron James. Greatness is exhausting every ounce of your ability and developing it to the highest level possible. If making the high school basketball team is the highest level you could reach with your ability, then that is greatness. Greatness is getting everything out of your ability that you can get. So many men barely scratch the surface of greatness and stay average their entire lives. Misery comes from knowing that you can be better even though you refuse to do what it takes to reach greatness. When a man is average, he is not a threat to the status quo. As men, we should shatter the status quo and set standards of greatness in everything we do. People look for the next great thing, not the next thing that falls into the average or standard category.

WAYS TO AVOID BEING AVERAGE

DEVELOP THE RIGHT MENTALITY.

In order to dodge being average, you've got to get and keep your mind right. You must have an "It's not over until I win" mentality. If you aren't resilient and able to bounce back from setbacks quickly, average will find you and hold you hostage. Eliminate negative words from your mentality, especially when referring to yourself. Affirm yourself daily and believe that you have what it takes to get the job done. When things go wrong, or you don't quite meet the mark, don't feel sorry for yourself. Be aggressive and jump back in the game. Never take defeat lying down. Refuse to take no for an answer, know what you want, and figure out how to go get it!

Having the right mentality will always keep you on attack mode in life. With the right mindset, average doesn't stand a chance against you.

GROW UP.

Choosing to mature is one of the greatest ways to ensure you never remain average. Maturing is a process, which means that you will always be observing your actions, thoughts, and productivity. With those things under a close radar, it's hard to settle for being average. As you mature, so many things will change about you.

A mature man says, "Pleasure can wait while I focus on what's important."

A mature man takes full responsibility for his actions.

A mature man takes criticism well and uses it to examine himself.

A mature man does not need to be validated by other people.

A mature man knows when to talk and when to keep quiet.

A mature man leads and does not follow.

A mature man seeks wise counsel before making a big decision.

A mature man can disagree without hate.

A mature man understands that God's timing is best.

A mature man can be trusted.

A mature man knows that putting down others will get him nowhere.

When a man has matured in his mind, attitude, and emotions, the little small, simple, and petty things in life are disregarded and do not hinder the vision for greatness he has for his life.

GET A MENTOR.

A great mentor will hold you accountable for not becoming average. Some men have a hard time receiving the assistance of mentors, especially those who did not have their fathers in their lives. However, having another man to guide you is necessary on your journey to greatness. Here are a few ways to know if a man could make a great mentor for you as you go after everything God has destined you to do and become.

Mentors are straightforward.
Mentors see things in you that you don't see in yourself.
Mentors can see when you are headed down a destructive path.
Mentors, in some cases, have been where you are headed.
Mentors look at the big picture, not just the right now.
Mentors are there to give you support.
Mentors can pull a positive out of any negative.
Mentors strengthen you when you feel fatigued.
Mentors are highly respected, and their presence demands respect.
Mentors motivate you so that you can accelerate past your current level.
Mentors play an important role in our lives. As men, we have to understand that we can't achieve greatness based on what we know and have experienced.

DON'T BE AFRAID TO TRY NEW THINGS.

We must be willing to step into new territory. The world we live in is constantly changing. We must transition with it, or we will become a thing of the past. Trying new things can be very uncomfortable because it causes you to change what you have been accustomed to and adjust to something new. Trying new things can set you up to be more successful than you have ever been in your life. Average people hate change... that's why they stay average.

OVERCOME PAST FAILURES AND THE MEMORIES THAT COME WITH THEM.

The memories of your past failures also bring about the emotions you felt in those moments. This can be a roadblock to stepping out and moving forward. Memories can spark positive emotions, but they can also bring about negative feelings. The emotions from your failures will cause you not to want to experience those failures ever again, causing you to not even try. As men, we cannot allow past failures and mistakes to keep us backed into a corner feeling defeated. We must come out fighting as if our lives depend on it.

After reading this chapter, I pray you believe that there is nothing average about you. Allow the wisdom and encouragement from this chapter to push you into your next level. People are waiting on you to go higher so that they can believe it is possible for them. Remember that staying average is selfish because it impacts everyone around you. There is greatness awaiting you, your friends, your family, your team, your employees, and even your enemies. Choose to be great!

NOTES

MESSAGE EIGHT

Fathers are Necessary

And you know that we treated each of you as a father treats his own children. We pleaded with you, encouraged you, and urged you to live your lives in a way that God would consider worthy. For he called you to share in his Kingdom and glory.

1 Thessalonians 2:11-12 (NLT)

Fatherhood requires unselfishness.
Fatherhood requires patience.
Fatherhood requires wisdom.
Fatherhood requires discernment.
Fatherhood requires courage.
Fatherhood requires you to be a provider.
Fatherhood requires you to be a protector.
Fatherhood requires you to be a visionary.

Fatherhood is the most challenging role a man will undertake. Fatherhood begins when conception takes place and doesn't end until you take your last breath. Wait a minute, did you say fatherhood begins at conception? Yes, sir. Fatherhood begins at conception because there has to be a time of preparation for the father, just as there is for the mother. A father must spend time preparing himself to raise a child even before the child is born. Once a man learns that he is to be a father, he must immediately start to change his way of thinking. When becoming a father, a man can no longer think about just himself. He must realize that the decisions he makes will affect the child also.

Fathers must realize that once their children become adults, their role is not done. It has actually just begun. Fathers are so important in the lives of their children. Fathers give identity to their children. Fathers provide counsel and impart strength to their children. Fathers give their children confidence. Fathers encourage their children when all hope is lost.

As a father, I always do my best to allow my kids to chose their own path in life. As fathers, we can sometimes have great expectations for our kids to become something they do not want to be. We may want our kids to be lawyers, doctors, business owners, or even athletes, and they may not want to go down the path that we envisioned for them. And it's okay.

As fathers, we must help our children develop good decision-making skills and allow them to choose their path because it is their life. Even if our children choose the wrong path, it is the father's responsibility to be there for support and to lend a helping hand. A father's love and support will do wonders for a child in whatever path they choose.

As a father, we cannot be prideful and only want our child to choose a path because it will make us proud. We must allow them to choose the path they feel is the purpose and direction for their life. At the end of the day, our children should be able to say that we were there when they needed us.

THE POWER, PRESENCE, AND PERSPECTIVE OF A FATHER POWER

A father can go to work, come home, wash the car, cut the grass, and make it all look effortless. A father can care for his wife and children and look good doing. A father can develop a strategy for a family trip or vacation, and everyone will have a good time. This is the power of a father. The power of a father is when he has the ability to get things done. Fathers have an innate ability to serve and care for their children like no other.

As men, we are the foundation of society. When men are not in their rightful place, society suffers. When fathers are not in their proper place in their children's lives, it negatively affects them beyond what the eye can see. When the father takes his rightful place in his children's lives, their sons will imitate what they see in generations to come, and their daughters will have high expectations from the men they choose as husbands.

PRESENCE

As a young boy, I would go to my friend's house during the day, and sometimes, his dad would not be home. When my friend's dad was not home, we felt like we could do whatever we wanted. However, when his dad was home, we knew we had to be on our best behavior. The father's presence at home prevents a lot of foolishness and misbehaving from taking place in their absence. The father commands respect from his children and others. The father's presence in homes would cut down on many behavior problems children and teenagers may be experiencing.

One out of every four children lives at home without their fathers. This causes a child not to consistently see the positive effect a father could have on their lives. Thus, making them feel like they don't need their father. This is dangerous because it could impact how they view men for the rest of their lives. The presence of a father prevents women and children from being taken advantage of. I understand the divorce factor and how it may impact the father's relationship with the children if the mother has sole custody. However, it is the father's responsibility to spend as much time as possible in his children's lives and positively influence them.

PERSPECTIVE

No matter what my kids may be going through or experiencing, I always want to show them a positive perspective or outlook in every situation. As a father, when you provide a positive perspective on your children's situation, this keeps the door open for future communication. When you always give your children negative feedback, they will refrain from coming to you for advice or wisdom. A father's negative words can leave children feeling wounded, while positivity will make children healthy and whole. The words of a father will either push a child away or pull them in closer. The words of a father carry life or death. Make sure that your children never feel torn down after talking with you. Build them up every chance you get. The words of a father will have a lifelong effect on children. As a father, make sure their memories of you are as positive as possible. How you speak to your child could influence how your children speak to their children. Fathers, we must set in motion words of life that will live beyond our last breath.

Fathers and fathers to be, you are necessary for the lives of your children. Never allow a court, individual, or a circumstance to convince you otherwise. Your children need more than your provision. There is so much power in your perspective and your presence. Do what it takes to be the father your children need you to be. If you never had a father in your life, glean from other fathers so that you will be the best father possible for your children. If you are reading this and have not been the best father, know that it is never too late to prioritize being in your child's life.

Again, the presence of the father changes everything about a child's life. Ensure that your presence is felt and positively impact the children God has blessed you with.

NOTES

MESSAGE NINE

Marriage is a Beautiful Thing

And the rib that the Lord God had taken from the man he made into a woman and brought her to the man. Then the man said, "This at last is bone of my bones and flesh of my flesh; she shall be called Woman, because she was taken out of Man." Therefore a man shall leave his father and his mother and hold fast to his wife, and they shall become one flesh.

Genesis 2:22-24 (ESV)

Ephesians 5:25 (ESV) says, "Husbands, love your wives, as Christ loved the church and gave himself up for her." Years ago, I asked a man who had been divorced if he would ever marry again, and he said no. Through conversations with him, I came to the conclusion that he did not want to get married again due to a broken heart. Many men think this way. After experienced a failed marriage, they convince themselves that it is safer to remain single and mingle. If you truly had your heart broken in a marriage or a relationship, it is a pain that you want to avoid for the rest of your life. Men will not come out and say it, but many men refuse to marry and become husbands because of the fear of their heart being shattered into pieces. Even if they find someone they truly love, marriage is still out of the question.

Another reason some men fear marriage is because they fear commitment. Many men have no desire to get married simply because they don't want to give up the freedom of being single. When you have been single and never had to share space, time, money, or food, it is very difficult to commit to sharing those things with another person for the rest of your life. Many men think long and hard about giving up what they call "freedom" to enter "bondage." Many men look at marriage as a lock down instead of a partnership.

WHEN YOU KNOW, YOU KNOW.

I remember the first time I met my wife. Within a few weeks of getting to know her, I knew she was the woman I would marry. How did I know? I can't really put it into words. It was just something I knew, deep down inside of me. I still went through the process of dating and getting engaged, but in reality, I knew she was the one right away. I was never afraid of getting my heart broken or committing to her. I wanted to be her husband, and I wanted her to be my wife. I was 23 when I married and was probably too young to be fearful of anything. Becoming a husband at such a young age, I did not know a lot of things that I wish I had learned. Nevertheless, I have enjoyed 24 years of marriage and counting. It gets better year after year. I am not talking fairy tale talk; I'm talking reality. It truly means a lot to me for my wife to carry my last name and call me her husband.

CHARACTERISTICS OF A GOOD HUSBAND

UNSELFISH

Being unselfish means being willing to deny yourself in order to cater to someone else. We live in a society in which we focus on ourselves and not others. Denying yourself to be a blessing to your wife is what being a husband is all about. As a single man coming into marriage, over time, that selfishness must be stripped away to truly be that husband your wife can be grateful for. When a man is willing to be unselfish towards his wife, his marriage will lack nothing. Why? Whatever a man gives his wife in seed form, his wife will return in harvest form. Whatever we give our wives, they are able to produce what we give them. When we give them sperm, they give us a child. When we give them groceries, they give us a meal. When we give them a house, they give us a home. You never lose out when you are selfless and put your wife first.

WATCHER

A good husband is a watcher. What is a watcher? A watcher is simply what a husband is to his wife. A watcher notices every detail and her routine. As you watch your wife in her daily routine, you can predict what she will do. When you can predict what she will do, you can know how to step in with a helping hand without her having to ask. This makes her heart glad. She understands that you have watched her to know how to help her. As a watcher, you notice changes to her hair, wardrobe, and most importantly, her countenance. As a husband, you should be able to discern by her countenance when something is bothering her. She shouldn't have to say anything. Your eyes should stay fixed on your wife through marriage, just like they were when you first met her.

LISTENER

So many marriages have failed simply because the husband or wife were not good listeners. Being a good listener reveals that you care about the welfare of the person talking. As husbands, we must be good listeners. We must allow our wives a safe space to express themselves without minimizing their feelings and cutting them off. Listening to your wife will tell you where she stands and where her heart is. Outside of God, we should be the person she can run to and reveal her thoughts and her heart's desire. As a husband, the last thing you want is for your wife to find others to share her heart with.

As husbands, we cannot be prideful and act like we have all the answers. We must be willing to show her how valuable she is by giving her undivided attention when she speaks. Remember, husband, if God connected you to her, you should seriously listen when she talks. Don't brush her off or ignore what she says. Your wife is able to tell you what friends you can and cannot trust. She can tell you when it is time to relax and take a break from the everyday pressures of life. Your wife can also give you insight into things that you think you have mastered. Wives are very discerning, and if we listen, they can keep us from making costly mistakes.

PROTECTOR

A protector is not just someone who will take a gun and defend his wife. A husband should protect his wife from the emotional and mental stress that could be detrimental to her health. Mental and emotional stress comes from kids, work, and being married. Even though God has blessed us with these things, they can easily become a burden if not managed properly. Husbands must be willing to protect their wives' mental and emotional state at all costs. Husbands must be willing to be inconvenienced and go the extra mile, so their wives don't have to. This will allow your wife to be at peace. Being a protector of your wife gives her a sense of restfulness that will truly benefit the marriage relationship. When the wife is calm and serene, it will be evident in the whole house.

VISIONARY

A visionary sees beyond the present state or condition of something or someone. Husbands should be able to look at their wives and not just see her for who she is, but who she can be. When you see potential in your wife, you must help her reach her potential in every possible way. Encourage your wife to pursue her purpose encouragingly. When a woman has the full support of her husband, there's no limit to what she can do. As a visionary to your wife, you can be the leading force in helping her become all that she has been purposed to become. As a visionary, you set the course for your wife to prevent distractions and keep deception from creeping into her life.

LOVE

Love your wife by freely and fully giving yourself to her. Loving your wife is not just about sexual intimacy. Loving your wife is catering to her needs, regardless of the commitment and the cost. John 3:16 says, "For God so loved the world that he gave his only begotten son that whosoever believes in him should not perish but have everlasting life."

God proved His love for us by giving his Son to die for us. Our love for our wives should be shown through how we give ourselves to them in every area of our lives. Make sure that you always give your wife your time, body, money, attention, words of encouragement, praise, respect, support in every endeavor, and everlasting love.

Marriage is serious, and it should not be taken lightly. However, it also not something you should fear as a man. God designed marriage not to hold you back as a man but to propel you forward. If your heart has been closed to the idea of marriage, pray and ask God to give you a new perspective. Yes, marriages have their challenges, but everything has a challenge. As a man, you aren't afraid of the challenge. Know that choosing marriage is a beautiful thing, and with the woman God has for you, it will benefit you more than you'll ever know.

NOTES

_____

_____

_____

_____

_____

_____

_____

_____

_____

_____

_____

_____

_____

_____

_____

_____

_____

_____

_____

_____

_____

_____

MESSAGE TEN

Be A Well-Rounded Man

*For everything there is a season, and a time for every matter under
heaven: a time to be born, and a time to die; a time to plant, and a
time to pluck up what is planted; a time to kill, and a time to heal; a
time to break down, and a time to build up; a time to weep, and a time
to laugh; a time to mourn, and a time to dance; a time to cast away
stones, and a time to gather stones together; a time to embrace, and a
time to refrain from embracing;*

Ecclesiastes 3:1-8 (ESV)

When we were in grade school, it seemed like every teacher asked us, "What do you want to be when you grow up?" Teachers asked this questions because they understood how essential careers would be once students graduated from high school. Our teachers also understood that at an early age, kids have the capability to dream freely, without fear of the factors that will come into play when they got older. Even though choosing a career path is important, I believe there are two other areas that make a man's life fulfilling: being part of and serving in church and being a positive role model in your community. Career, church, and community are three areas I believe men should launch themselves into in order to be well-rounded individuals. Let's discuss the importance of each one.

CAREER

Our career is our personal, individual pursuit of what we desire to contribute to society. Our careers are what we spend most of our time on during the day, especially during the week. We go to school or attend special training programs to elevate our knowledge of the career that we choose. Our careers can set us up and make us financially secure in the years to come. Our careers give us an identity and respectability in the arena that we choose to pursue. If we are going to be successful in our chosen career, we must be willing to make personal sacrifices, allot the necessary time to learn our field, and have good prioritizing skills.

PERSONAL SACRIFICE

If you are going to succeed at anything in life, you must be willing to make sacrifices. When pursuing and maintaining a career, personal sacrifice is a must. Personal sacrifice requires a certain level of maturity. Personal sacrifice is when you can put off pleasure for today in order to experience success for tomorrow. Personal sacrifice is hours upon hours of working, studying, planning, and thinking when others are enjoying fun activities. I'm not speaking against having a good time. However, you must be disciplined enough to know that there is a time for work and a time for play. Unfortunately, many have not been able to balance play and work. As a result, they never reach their full potential in their career.

TIME ALLOTMENT

If you ever have an opportunity to sit down with a successful person, they will tell you that time allotment or time management is one of the keys to their many accomplishments. Time allotment is setting aside time for a particular purpose or task. During the offseason, getting ready for football, I would always set aside time to workout. These workout times would vary but were never compromised. When you believe in the career path that you choose, you must exhibit a level of focus and seriousness in order to be successful. Time is easily wasted if you allow it to be wasted. Setting aside time to develop your craft could be the difference between average and great. Wasted time will lead to wasted development. Wasted development will lead to closed doors of opportunity. Take advantage of the time that you have to develop in your career path. Trust me; it will pay big dividends in the future.

PROPERLY PLACED PRIORITIES

What is most important in our lives should be first place

in our lives. Yes, your career is important. However, you must have a well-balanced spiritual, family, social, and career life. Even though your career is important, it can be here today and gone tomorrow. When your career is done, what will you have left? It is important to have your priorities in place. We can prioritize our lives however we see fit, but here is an example that might benefit you.

1. Your relationship with God (includes the will of God and serving in church)
2. Your wife (if married)
3. Your family
4. Your career
5. Your personal enjoyment
6. Your friendships

Your list may be different, but you cannot allow misplaced priorities to rob you of a successful career and a joyous life outside of your career.

CHURCH

I truly believe that homes, schools, and churches should be full of strong, committed, and reliable men. When strong men are in schools, homes, and churches, it strengthens those institutions altogether. When women and children are accustomed to seeing men in their rightful places, it gives them a sense of security. I believe there is nothing more powerful than a man of God serving and being committed to a local church. When a man is committed to serving in a local church, it reveals that he is not just concerned with satisfying himself but catering to the needs of others. When a man regularly attends a local church, there is a higher possibility that he can be trusted over time. I know some of you are saying, "Well, there are some devilish men who go to church." And, you are right.

In the world, there are both good and bad things. We see this in every environment we encounter. Nowhere is perfect. However, choose to look at the positives, brother.

When it comes to church, think about the men who prove what hearing the preached word can do for your life, if applied. Men that serve in their local church inspire and influence other men to follow suit.

For some men, going to church is not a manly thing to do. I will be the first to testify that going to church will make you an even stronger man. Going to church will cause you to see where you fall short and how you can become better. When the man goes to church, more than likely, his wife and children will follow, causing the family to be rooted and grounded in God.

COMMUNITY

As a kid, I participated in a lot of youth league sports that were coached by men from my community. These men were not paid financially but were paid by the positive impact the young boys made as they grew older. The men in our community had jobs and families but chose to spend precious time coaching and mentoring young kids in their community. I went on to play high school, college, and professional sports, and I know the success of my athletic career was because of their impact on my life. You may not be a coach, but you can be a positive influence in your community. You can do yard work for the elderly in your community or be a blessing to the less fortunate. Your community goes beyond the street that you live on, but it spreads throughout the whole city.

Cities are in need of positive males, regardless of the role you play. Men can be positive role models to the young men who are growing up without their fathers. I truly believe that if more men took the time and the initiative to mentor one young man, it would make the world of a difference. Society would benefit greatly if more men would reach out to their communities on purpose and lend a hand where they are so desperately needed.

Throughout this book, we have discussed many topics, all of which are vital to you understanding the value of being a man. There are so many books available to women, but there are not a lot of resources available to help men. I wrote this book to share the wisdom that I've gained throughout my life to men who may not have had any male guidance. I pray that this book has helped you to understand your purpose as a man. When you turn the last page, my prayer is that you would dive headfirst into purpose and experience every good thing God has planned for you.

As men, we naturally give attention to what we can physically see, but I hope this book has impacted you beyond what you can see in the mirror. I hope this book has encouraged your heart to try again, despite the failures you may have experienced. I hope this book has encouraged you to invest more time in your visions, goals, and dreams. I hope that this book has inspired you to seek God's restoration. More than anything, I hope that after reading this book, your life will never be the same.

You are a man. You are powerful. You are needed. You

are necessary. Don't let anyone tell you otherwise. Don't keep this book to yourself. Share this message with every man you encounter.

Acknowledgments

For years, my wife, Candice, suggested I write a book. I am so grateful to her for believing that I could do this. I dedicate this book to her and our amazing children, Desiree', Kendall, and Caleb. I am so thankful that God has blessed me with a family who supports me in everything I do.

I would like to say a big thank you to my parents, John and Ruby Hayes, for the love and Christ-like home environment I grew up in. I appreciate my brother Derrick and sisters, Patricia and Renita, for the support they have shown me through out my life.

To my pastors, Pastor Darius and Alesia Crayton, thank you for guiding me as I grow and develop in my walk with God. Thank you for giving me the opportunity to serve in ministry.

There are many others who have contributed to making me the man I am today. To each of you, thank you. I love and appreciate you from the bottom of my heart.

Meet the Author

High school athletics led Jarius Hayes to a stellar collegiate football career at the University of North Alabama. He received numerous awards and accomplishments to include, three time NCCA Division II All American (1993-1996) and three NCCA Division II National Championships. He is an inductee in both The University of North Alabama Hall of Fame and Colbert County Hall of Fame. He was afforded the opportunity to play in the NFL with the Arizona Cardinals and The NFL European League/Amsterdam.

Following football, he found a new passion working with youth and young adult men in one of the largest detention centers in Phoenix, Arizona. He has extensive training in crisis intervention, anger management, behavior disorders, and substance abuse issues.

Jarius is married to his lovely wife of twenty-four years, Candice Hayes. They have three adult children, a son-in-law, and two grandchildren.

His life's mission is to inspire and encourage individuals to make an impact and make a positive change in the lives of men.

Stay Connected

Thank you for reading, *A Message to the Man*. Jarius looks forward to connecting with you. Here are a few ways you can connect with the author and stay updated on new releases, speaking engagements, products, and more.

FACEBOOK	JAIRUS HAYES
INSTAGRAM	@jariushayes84
TWITTER	@HayesJarius
WEBSITE	www.jariushayes.com
EMAIL	admin@jariushayes.com

www.ingramcontent.com/pod-product-compliance
Lightning Source LLC
LaVergne TN
LVHW011337080426
835513LV00006B/402